I0105614

SO, YOU WANT A
GREEN CARD?

U.S. Immigration Lawyer With Millions Of Youtube Views Reveals Her Secrets And Tips For Getting A Green Card

By

Anne Zeitoun-Sedki

U.S. Immigration Attorney

Copyright © 2025 by Anne Zeitoun-Sedki

All rights reserved. No part of this publication may be reproduced, distributed, or transmitted in any form or by any means, including photocopying, recording, or other electronic or mechanical methods, without the prior written permission of the publisher, except in the case of brief quotations embodied in critical reviews and certain other noncommercial uses permitted by copyright law.

Published by Hemingway publisher

Cover design by Hemingway Publisher

ISBN: Printed in the United States

HEMINGWAY
PUBLISHERS

Table of Contents

Dedication

To my incredible family

To my parents, whose love and sacrifices built the foundation of everything I am.

To my husband, whose patience, encouragement, and belief in me never wavered.

To my sister, my confidante and constant source of strength.

And to my children, the light of my life, who inspire me to grow, learn, and lead with purpose.

Your love, sacrifices, and encouragement have shaped both the person and the advocate I've become.

A heartfelt thank you to Attorney Nader Anise; your mentorship and persistent encouragement pushed me to write this book. Your belief in the importance of sharing my voice, vision, and expertise gave me the courage to share my story and knowledge with the world. Thank you for seeing the potential in me before I saw it in myself.

With deep appreciation,
— *Anne Zeitoun-Sedki*

Introduction

Purpose Of The Handbook

This book is intended to serve as a guide that helps you navigate a complex and ever-changing immigration system, without losing your sanity or your place in line. In it, I will share the experience and insight I have gained since I began practicing law in 2008. As an experienced immigration lawyer, I have seen firsthand the challenges, uncertainties, and complexities that individuals and families face when navigating the U.S. immigration system. This handbook is designed to serve as a practical guide, providing clear, reliable, and up-to-date information to help you understand your rights, options, and responsibilities under immigration law.

If you are seeking to apply for legal permanent residency (also known as a green card), this book will break down key legal concepts into clear and understandable language. You don't need a law degree, a legal dictionary(well, maybe sometimes) or a gallon of coffee to make sense of it. While no handbook can (or should) replace personalized legal advice, my goal is to empower you with the knowledge that will help you make informed decisions and avoid common pitfalls.

Immigration laws and policies are constantly evolving, and misinformation can have serious consequences. I have seen cases derailed over something as small as a wrong checkbox. Don't let that be you. This guide is designed to clarify procedures, outline potential legal pathways, and provide insights based on years of experience representing clients from diverse backgrounds.

I encourage you to use this handbook as a starting point in your journey and to seek professional legal counsel when necessary. **This book is not intended to take the place of an experienced immigration attorney**. An informed immigrant is an empowered immigrant, and I'm hopeful that this resource helps you move forward with confidence.

Welcome to your pathway to the American Dream.

Let's begin this journey together!

Overview of the U.S. Immigration System

The U.S. immigration system is extremely complex, and the process for obtaining a green card can throw you into a whirlwind (a dark hole of endless delays!) if you don't fully understand which process you are applying for and how to apply. Picture a maze where the walls keep shifting, except the prize at the end is your legal status, not a block of cheese.

The process varies depending on the type of green card you are applying for, whether it's family-sponsored, employment-based, through the Diversity Visa Lottery, or other special categories, such as via asylum or refugee status. This handbook is designed to guide you through the various pathways to obtaining a green card, from understanding eligibility requirements to preparing your application and navigating the interview process. And yes, we will also cover how to handle the nail-biting waiting periods without refreshing your case tracker every five minutes.

Each chapter will delve into specific aspects of the green card process, providing detailed information, practical tips, and resources to help you navigate your journey. My goal is to simplify this information and process as much as possible, and provide you with practical, straightforward advice.

PLEASE NOTE: Immigration law is subject to frequent changes. While I have attempted to provide you with the most up-to-date laws and information, there may still be a possibility that new regulations. Therefore, it is always wise to schedule a consultation with an immigration attorney to discuss your particular case.

Before we delve into the 'meat' of the process, here is my first and ultimately my most important tip, which we'll call the PRO TIP. It will be relevant throughout each chapter of this book and throughout your entire immigration journey to obtaining a green card.

Ready? ... here it is:

💡 **Pro Tip:** START EARLY AND STAY ORGANIZED

Starting early and staying organized isn't just about reducing stress—it's about making sure that you don't miss critical steps or deadlines. The immigration process can be unpredictable, but your preparation doesn't have to be.

Here's how to do that:

1. **Start Early:** Immigration applications often require extensive documentation, including birth certificates, proof of relationship, financial records, and other supporting documents. Getting a head start gives you plenty of time to gather everything you need and helps you avoid last-minute scrambling if you discover a missing document or face delays.

2. **Create a System:** Keep your paperwork organized by establishing a clear filing system, whether digital or physical. Use labeled

folders for each document category (e.g., "Passport Copies," "Medical Exam Records," "Affidavit of Support"). Store any correspondence with immigration authorities in a dedicated folder.

3. **Track Deadlines:** Immigration forms often have strict deadlines, and missing them can delay your application process or result in its rejection. Use a calendar or task management tool to track submission dates, required follow-ups, and expiration dates (like medical exams or police certificates)

4. **Double-Check Requirements:** The forms and supporting documents required can vary depending on the type of application you're filing. Please review the instructions for each form carefully and ensure that you meet all the requirements before submitting. This can save you from costly mistakes and the need to refile later.

5. **Keep Copies of Everything:** Always make photocopies or digital scans of everything you submit. Immigration authorities can sometimes lose documents or request additional information, and having a complete record on hand can expedite the process.

6. **Stay Updated:** Immigration laws and forms are subject to frequent changes. Regularly check the official immigration website (such as USCIS in the U.S.) to stay informed about updates, new forms, or changes in fees. It's also a good idea to sign up for email notifications if available. In immigration, 'I didn't know' is never an acceptable excuse, so stay in the loop.

Chapter 1
Understanding the Green Card

What is a Green Card?

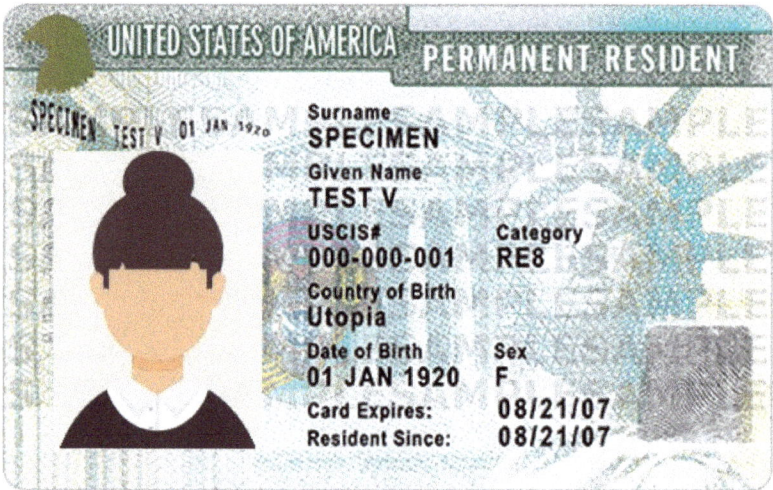

Well, it's what everyone dreams of when they think of the United States! It's the golden ticket for a new life. But what is an actual green card? A green card, officially known as a Permanent Resident Card, is a document issued by the United States Citizenship and Immigration Services (USCIS) that grants non-U.S. citizens the right to live and work permanently in the United States. Holding a green card signifies that you have been granted lawful permanent residency (GREEN CARD HOLDER) in the U.S.

Throughout my years of practice, I would say that my favorite moment in representing my clients is the reaction I get when they receive their green card for the first time. It is almost always accompanied by tears of happiness, which usually make me tear up. It's the moment they've been waiting for, usually after many years, and I am always happy to share it with my clients. It's the beginning of a new life for them, and another reason I keep doing what I'm doing.

With the green card comes many benefits. These include the ability to work for any employer and access to government benefits, such as Social Security benefits, government-sponsored healthcare, and educational assistance. Think of it as unlocking the 'full-access' version of life in America, without the constant worry of visa expiration dates hanging over your head. As a green card holder, you get travel flexibility, which means you can travel freely in and out of the U.S. without needing to apply for a visa every time you travel. Of course, there are limitations, which we will discuss in the next section regarding the responsibilities of green card holders.

Being a green card holder also provides you with many of the legal rights as U.S. citizens, like due process and protection under the law. You can also sponsor other family members for a green card, specifically a spouse or an unmarried child who is under or above the age of 21.

Most importantly, it is the pathway to U.S. Citizenship! typically, after five (or three) years as a green card holder, you are eligible to apply for U.S. citizenship through a process called naturalization. That's when the dream gets its final stamp of approval: you can vote, get a U.S. passport, and no longer have to explain to airport immigration why you are carrying a green card instead of a blue booklet. So, this is the crucial step to a new life in the U.S. We will discuss this in a later chapter, but for now, I am sharing the best ways to obtain a green card and how to maintain it.

Overview of pathways to a green card

Before delving into how to apply, you must understand which green card process you are applying for. Think of it like choosing the right lane on a highway, pick the wrong one and you might end up in Canada. Each process is uniquely different from the other, so having a clear understanding of which green card path you're taking will make all the difference.

First, if you plan to apply for a green card for yourself or someone else *on your own,* which I highly advise against, due to the potential for errors that can occur along the way, I suggest you find the proper resources for your information. Relying on "advice" from friends, family, or community members can be detrimental to your case, costing you a significant amount of money and time, and potentially preventing you from ever obtaining a green card.

I have seen it happen all too often just because a client decided to file their case on their own. Sometimes they walk into my office with a denial letter and the same look you get when you realize you've been microwaving your coffee in the wrong mug. So, BEWARE of doing it alone.

The #1 reason people decide to file on their own instead of through an experienced immigration attorney: the **cost.** Many people tell me the reason they didn't go through an attorney was the cost of attorney fees. However, what most people fail to realize is that the cost to fix a case, after errors are made and the case is denied, is significantly higher due to attorney fees. It's the legal version of buying a $20 "cheap" printer, then spending $200 on ink. So, what most people think they are initially "saving", they end up spending far more to fix avoidable errors.

The lesson: find an experienced immigration attorney!

(Hint – my contact information is available in the back of this book.)

However, as the old saying goes, *"You can lead a horse to water, but you can't make it drink!"* And in immigration, you can lead someone to an attorney's office, but you can't stop them from Googling "shortcuts" at midnight.

So, if you plan on filing your case on your own, here's my tip:

> 💡 **Tip: Avoid misinformation by relying on official sources**

Once you have determined which green card pathway you will choose, locate the appropriate resource for your case. You will find the links to these official sources at the end of this handbook, but here are some sources you should turn to for the right information:

➢ U.S. Citizenship and Immigration Services (USCIS) – for practically any case you're filing

- ➢ Department of State – if you're filing your case through an Embassy or Consulate
- ➢ Department of Labor – if you're filing an employment-based green card
- ➢ Executive Office of Immigration Review (EOIR) – if you're in deportation proceedings in the Immigration Court

> 💡 **Tip: Research which pathway is best suited for your situation.**

There are typically five ways to get a green card:

1. Through immediate family members
2. Employment sponsorship
3. An investment,
4. A humanitarian status,
5. Through other special situations.

Here they are:

1. Family-Based Green Card

This is one of the most common ways to obtain a green card, allowing U.S. citizens and permanent residents to sponsor their close family members. It is also the most confusing for most of my clients.

Some think 'immediate family' includes cousins twice removed and that one uncle they see at weddings, spoiler alert: it doesn't.

In the following two categories, you will see that the listed "immediate" family members of U.S. citizens are exempt from a visa cap. This means the green card is available for them, and there is generally no long wait time for them to obtain the green card.

Who is considered an "immediate family member?"

> ➢ Spouses

> ➢ Unmarried children under 21

> ➢ Parents (if the U.S. citizen is over 21)

The 'Marriage Green Card'

So, you've found a spouse who loves you and you're ready to start your new life together in the U.S. Congratulations! But before you start planning your Thanksgiving dinners with the in-laws, you'll need to tackle one little thing: the paperwork. Think of it like a wedding, but skip the champagne, the dancing, and the cake. What do you get instead? Forms. Endless forms.

The 'Marriage Green Card' is one of the most common ways to obtain a green card in the United States. This process is available to foreign nationals who marry a U.S. citizen or lawful permanent resident. While the idea of a "marriage-based green card " sounds straightforward, the process can be intricate, requiring both the applicant and their U.S. spouse to prove the legitimacy of their marriage. It's almost always the first thing clients ask me about because the process can be a *faster* route to permanent residency compared to other immigration pathways. However, it's essential to approach it carefully. Fraudulent marriages, or those entered into solely for the purpose of obtaining a green card, can result in severe penalties, including denial of the application, deportation, and even criminal charges.

To qualify, the marriage must be legally valid, and the couple must demonstrate that their relationship is genuine and not one entered into solely for immigration benefits. The U.S. citizen or permanent resident spouse must file a petition (Form I-130) to sponsor their foreign spouse, and the foreign spouse must apply to adjust their status (Form I-485) if they are already in the U.S. or apply for a visa through consular processing if they are outside the U.S.

Once the petition is approved, the foreign spouse will receive their green card after an interview with U.S. Citizenship and Immigration Services (USCIS), where both spouses may be asked questions about their relationship. This is not the time to realize you've never actually discussed who takes out the trash. If the marriage is less than two years old at the time of approval, the foreign spouse will receive a **conditional green card** valid for two years. After this period, they can apply to remove the conditions and obtain a permanent green card.

> ⚠ **Disclaimer:** The names used in the following incidence have been changed to maintain the privacy of the individuals discussed.

A few years ago, I had a client (let's say her name was "Rosa") who was marrying "David", a U.S. citizen. Rosa had come to the U.S. from Colombia on a student visa, and she and David had met through mutual friends. They quickly fell in love and decided to get married. Naturally, they wanted to ensure the book did everything, so they called my office for an initial consultation, made an appointment, and came to me for guidance on applying for Rosa's Marriage Green Card.

Rosa was a bit nervous about the process, especially the interview. She had heard horror stories about how intense and uncomfortable these interviews could be. (You know, the kind where the officer allegedly stares you down like you just tried to smuggle a llama through customs.) But she and David had been together for almost two years, and their marriage was the real deal. They were both confident in their relationship, but she couldn't help but feel anxious about what questions they would be asked.

As the interview day approached, we went over everything—what to expect, how to respond, and what documentation to bring. I explained to Rosa that the interviewer's job was to verify the legitimacy of the marriage, and they might ask questions about how they met, where they went on their first date, and how they spent their time together. I even joked, "Don't be surprised if they ask you about your favorite ice cream flavor." It was a bit of a light-hearted comment, but from my experience, I knew that type of question wasn't inconceivable.

The big day arrived, and I gave them a final word of encouragement: "Relax, just be yourselves, and it'll be fine."

Hours later, I received a call from Rosa, and her voice was filled with both excitement and disbelief.

"Anne, they asked me what my favorite ice cream was!" she exclaimed.

I couldn't help but laugh. "Told you!"

Apparently, the interviewer had asked both Rosa and David a series of "get-to-know-you" questions. They were asked about their daily routines, their favorite activities, and yes, they even had a lengthy discussion about their ice cream preferences. Rosa's was vanilla, David's was chocolate chip, and the couple had laughed through the whole thing. The officer's goal wasn't to get the "right" answer; it was to see if they knew these seemingly small details about each other, to gauge if their relationship was genuine.

In the end, their green card was approved without any issues. It turns out that the question about ice cream was more than just a quirky interview moment. It was a way for the officer to assess their familiarity with each other and the comfort of their bond. Rosa and David had nothing to worry about. They were clearly a couple that had shared many small moments, including their favorite desserts.

> 💡 **Tip:** Be proactive and include more documentation than you think you need. Instead of just submitting the minimum requirement, consider including additional proof, such as joint utility bills, insurance policies, photos from holidays or family events, and even affidavits from friends and family attesting to the authenticity of your relationship. The more evidence you have, the stronger your case will be, showing that your marriage is genuine and not just for immigration purposes.

For this second category, these individuals are faced with a visa cap, which means, depending on their group, they must wait a certain period before they are eligible to apply for a green card. Let's break it down:

- **Family Preference Categories** (subject to annual caps and waiting times):

  - ➤ F-1: Unmarried children over 21 of U.S. citizens

  - ➤ F-2A: Spouses and children (under 21) of permanent residents

  - ➤ F-2B: Unmarried children (over 21) of permanent residents

  - ➤ F-3: Married children of U.S. Citizens

  - ➤ F-4: Brothers and sisters of U.S. citizens (only if the U.S. citizen is over 21)

Family-Sponsored	All Chargeability Areas Except Those Listed	CHINA-mainland born	INDIA	MEXICO	PHILIPPINES
F1	22NOV15	22NOV15	22NOV15	22NOV04	08MAR12
F2A	01JAN22	01JAN22	01JAN22	15MAY21	01JAN22
F2B	22MAY16	22MAY16	22MAY16	01JUL05	22OCT11
F3	01JUL10	01JUL10	01JUL10	22NOV00	08NOV02
F4	01AUG07	01AUG07	08APR06	01MAR01	01MAY04

How to read the visa bulletin:

As you can see, China, India, Mexico, and the Philippines have their own separate categories. All other countries follow the first column. Yes, even if you've been in the U.S. long enough to forget that most of the world doesn't do month/day/year. You read the date as follows: day, month, year. So, for example:

If you are a U.S. citizen applying for your unmarried child over the age of 21 who is living in Spain, you would consult the chart below for the F-1 category in the first column, which shows a date of 22nd November 2015. This means that if you filed a family petition for your child today, that child would have to wait approximately 10 years (2025-2015) to apply for a green card, since that is when the green card would be available. That's enough time for them to finish med school, learn French, and binge every episode of "The Office" twice.

In another example, if you are a green card holder and would like to sponsor your husband or wife for a green card (F2) and they are living in China, your spouse would need to wait approximately three years to be eligible for the green card (2025-2022)

Visa Bulletin for February 2025 (changes every month)

Family-Sponsored	All Chargeability Areas Except Those Listed	CHINA-mainland born	INDIA	MEXICO	PHILIPPINES
F1	22NOV15	22NOV15	22NOV15	22NOV04	08MAR12
F2A	01JAN22	01JAN22	01JAN22	15MAY21	01JAN22
F2B	22MAY16	22MAY16	22MAY16	01JUL05	22OCT11
F3	01JUL10	01JUL10	01JUL10	22NOV00	08NOV02
F4	01AUG07	01AUG07	08APR06	01MAR01	01MAY04

💡 **Tip: Don't wait to file the I-130 petition! The filing of the petition locks in your "priority date." The priority date is like your relative's ticket in line and will secure their place in line until they can file for a green card.**

2. Employment-Based Green Card

Employment-based green cards are granted to individuals who have job offers from U.S. employers or who possess extraordinary skills in certain fields. There are several categories based on the level of skill and job requirements.

Categories:

➢ **EB-1**: For individuals with extraordinary abilities in fields like science, arts, business, or athletics, outstanding professors/ researchers or multinational executives/ managers.

➢ **EB-2**: For professionals with advanced degrees or exceptional abilities in fields such as science, engineering, or business.

➢ **EB-3**: For skilled workers (jobs requiring at least 2 years of training or experience), professionals (with a bachelor's degree), and other workers (for jobs not requiring formal qualifications).

➢ **EB-4**: For special immigrants like religious workers, employees of international organizations, or certain other groups.

➢ **EB-5**: For immigrant investors who invest a minimum of $800,000 in a U.S. business that creates at least 10 full-time jobs for U.S. workers.

Employment-based	All Chargeability Areas Except Those Listed	CHINA-mainland born	INDIA	MEXICO	PHILIPPINES
1st	C	01JAN23	15APR22	C	C
2nd	01AUG23	01OCT20	01JAN13	01AUG23	01AUG23
3rd	01MAR23	15NOV20	08JUN13	01MAR23	01MAR23
Other Workers	22MAY21	01JAN18	08JUN13	22MAY21	22MAY21
4th	01FEB21	01FEB21	01FEB21	01FEB21	01FEB21
Certain Religious Workers	01FEB21	01FEB21	01FEB21	01FEB21	01FEB21
5th Unreserved (including C5, T5, I5, R5)	C	01OCT16	01APR22	C	C
5th Set Aside: (Rural - 20%)	C	C	C	C	C
5th Set Aside: (High Unemployment - 10%)	C	C	C	C	C
5th Set Aside: (Infrastructure - 2%)	C	C	C	C	C

This bulletin is only being used for illustration purposes and does not reflect the current processing times.

Contrary to popular opinion, the immigration attorney's job is not to find you an employer. (Professional headhunters do that best.) Suppose you are seeking an employment-based green card. In that case, it is essential to approach your attorney prepared with the employer who is willing to sponsor you, along with a clear understanding of the job position and duties you are expected to hold within that company/business. Having that information ready will ensure the process goes smoothly and effectively.

3. Diversity Visa Lottery (Green Card Lottery)

The Diversity Immigrant Visa Program—also known as the Green Card Lottery—is like the Powerball of immigration, except instead of winning cash, you win the right to spend the next few years filling out paperwork and learning what a "Form DS-260" is. Each year, it randomly awards up to 55,000 green cards to people from countries with low immigration rates to the U.S.

Eligibility

➤ Applicants must be from eligible countries (those that have sent fewer than 50,000 immigrants to the U.S. in the past five years).

➤ Applicants must meet minimum education or work experience requirements (usually at least a high school diploma or two years of work experience in an eligible occupation).

4. Refugee or Asylum Status

Suppose you have been granted asylum or admitted to the United States as a refugee. In that case, you may be eligible to apply for a green card after one year of being in the U.S. Refugees are required by law to apply for a green card one year after their arrival, while asylees have the option but are strongly encouraged to do so. It's essential to verify that you meet all eligibility requirements, including not having resettled in another country or committed certain crimes, as these may impact your application.

Categories:

➤ Refugees are individuals who are outside their home country due to fear of persecution and are admitted to the U.S. for humanitarian reasons.

➤ Asylees are individuals already in the U.S. who fear persecution in their home country and seek protection in the U.S.

5. Special Immigrants

Certain special categories of individuals are eligible for a green card under specific conditions. These include:

- ➢ **U Visa**: For victims of certain crimes who have helped law enforcement with investigations or prosecutions.

- ➢ **T Visa**: For victims of human trafficking who assist in investigations.

- ➢ **SIJ (Special Immigrant Juveniles)**: For children who have been abused, abandoned, or neglected by one or both parents.

- ➢ **Religious Workers**: Religious ministers or those working in religious occupations can apply for a green card under the EB-4 category.

In the next chapter, we will discuss the details and process for each category. Still, it is essential to know which pathway you will begin and determine who will be the *Petitioner*—the one filing the petition/application—and who will be the *Beneficiary*—the one receiving the benefit, or in this context, the green card.

Generally, in each of these processes, there are four main steps:

1. **Petitioning**: The applicant (or a family member, employer, or qualifying organization) files a petition on their behalf (e.g., Form I-130, Form I-140).

2. **Wait for Visa Availability**: Some categories, such as family-based and employment-based green cards, require applicants to wait for a visa number to become available due to annual limits. The wait time varies based on the category and country of origin.

3. **Application**: Once a visa number is available, the applicant can apply for a green card through adjustment of status (if in the U.S.) or consular processing (if outside the U.S.).

4. **Interview and Approval**: The applicant may be required to undergo an interview, submit biometrics, and provide additional documentation before the green card is granted.

Again, we will delve into this further later, but for now, once you know which pathway you will begin, we need to decide whether the green card can be applied for from within the U.S. or outside the U.S. through a U.S. Embassy or Consulate. This is discussed in the coming chapter.

Keep going!

Chapter 2
Navigating the Application Process

The Key Forms and Supporting Documents Needed

The journey to obtaining a U.S. green card —a permanent resident card—is a significant and often complex process. For many, the ultimate goal is the ability to live and work in the United States without worrying about visa limitations or deportation. But navigating the various paths to a green card can feel overwhelming, especially when you're unsure which route applies to your specific situation.

Whether you're seeking a green card through family ties, employment, asylum, or marriage, understanding the available options is crucial to making the right decisions along the way. Each path has its own set of requirements, documentation, and processes, and the journey can vary greatly depending on your circumstances.

Let's discuss the steps of filing in each one.

1. Family-Based Green Card

The U.S. citizen or permanent resident (the sponsor) files **Form I-130** with **USCIS** to establish the relationship between them and the family member they are sponsoring. You can do this by filing a paper application with the USCIS Service Center or online if you create a USCIS account. I have always been old school and preferred the old-fashioned paper filing, but with the increasing backlogs at USCIS AND increased filing fees for paper-filing, I am more inclined to tell my clients to create a USCIS account and file online. This has proven (so far) to result in a faster processing time, and you have access to all your documents and receipts through the USCIS account, reducing the risk of losing important paperwork.

Supporting Documents: You'll need to provide documents proving the following:

➤ The sponsor's status (copy of your U.S. passport, birth certificate, or green card)

➤ Your relationship, such as birth certificates, marriage certificates, or adoption record

---

💡 **Tip:** Foreign documents must be in the proper format acceptable by the Department of State and must be properly translated if not provided in a bilingual format.

The review of the I-130 petition can take several months (often 6-12 months or longer, depending on the specific case and the USCIS service center).

> 💡 **Tip:** If the relative is in the U.S. and eligible for adjustment of status (AOS), the sponsor can file the I-130 at the same time as the I-485 (green card application)

If USCIS approves the petition, and the relative is outside the U.S they'll forward the case to the **National Visa Center (NVC)** for consular processing (discussed more in the next section)

You will receive a receipt notice that contains important information that you will need to keep handy, so make sure you save that I-130 receipt in a safe spot! The receipt notice will contain the name of the Petitioner and Beneficiary, but more importantly, it will contain the 'Priority date' that will be very important if you need to consult the visa bulletin for processing times and to know when the Beneficiary is eligible for a green card.

> 💡 **Tip:** Make sure all the information on the receipt is correct. If any errors, make sure to correct them as soon as possible with USCIS.

2. Employment-Based Green Card

Employment-based green cards are handled much differently from family-based green cards. The process involves multiple steps, and it typically takes longer than family-based petitions due to labor certification requirements and other factors. Labor Certification is required for most EB-2 and EB-3 green card applicants and is filed through the **PERM** (Program Electronic Review Management) process. This step ensures that there are no qualified U.S. workers available for the position and that hiring a foreign worker will not negatively affect U.S. workers' wages or working conditions.

Typically, the employee who is being sponsored for the green card is not involved at all in the initial steps of this process. It is mainly the employer going through several different steps to demonstrate to the Department of Labor that they have attempted to find a suitable candidate for a job position, but couldn't, and need the employee/ beneficiary to fill that position in the company.

> 💡 **Tip:** Before starting this process, make sure the employer is legally compliant with all state and federal regulations.

So, here are the steps the employer must take

1. **Employer's Responsibility**: The employer must file a Labor Certification with the U.S. Department of Labor (DOL).

    - The employer must demonstrate that they conducted a recruitment process (advertising the job and attempting to hire U.S. workers).

    - This includes posting the job internally, advertising in newspapers, and potentially using job fairs.

2. **Recruitment Process**: The employer must document the recruitment efforts and demonstrate that no qualified U.S. workers were available for the position.

3. **PERM Filing**: If no qualified U.S. workers are found, the employer can submit the PERM application to the DOL through the ETA Form 9089.

4. **DOL Review**: The DOL will review the PERM application, and if approved, the employer will receive Labor Certification approval.

Once the Labor certification is approved, the Employer is now able to begin the actual green card filing for the employee (and family members) by filing the I-140 petition with USCIS.

3. Diversity Lottery Program

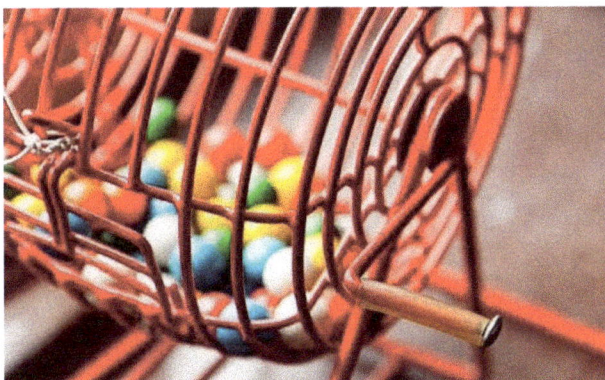

The Diversity Visa Lottery, also known as the Green Card Lottery, aims to diversify the immigrant population in the United States by selecting applicants from countries with low rates of immigration to the U.S. Each year, up to 50,000 visas are awarded through a random drawing.

Just like its name, this pathway is a lottery, and it's a completely random selection process, so there is absolutely no guarantee of getting selected. If you are one of the lucky ones, the process doesn't stop at registration. You have to see it all the way through and make sure you're doing it correctly

Let's walk through the steps:

1. Make sure you're eligible to apply.

➢ You must be a native of a qualifying country

➢ You must meet certain education or work experience criteria

2. Go to the website and submit an application.

➢ Make sure you apply during the application period (usually one month in the fall)

➢ Make sure all of the information on the application is correct

➢ Include ALL your family members- you won't be able to add them later if they were already born at the time of submitting your application

➢ Save the application confirmation number in a safe place! (You can't retrieve it anywhere on the website.)

💡 **Tip:** Submit only one application per person. Multiple entries will disqualify you from the program.

💡 **Tip:** ALWAYS use the right website to register to avoid immigration scams! The DV lottery is FREE, so you shouldn't pay for it! https://dvprogram.state.gov

---

3. Prepare a valid, unexpired passport.

4. Use the confirmation number to check the status of your application through the official website (usually in May of the following year).

> 💡 **Tip:** No notification will be sent by mail. If you receive an email or a mail, it's a scam!

5. Prepare for the next steps (If selected).

➢ If you are selected, you will need to go through further steps such as submitting documents, attending a visa interview, and undergoing a medical examination.

➢ Be prepared for the consular interview with all required documentation (passport, educational and work records, etc.).

6. Stay updated.

➢ Always check the U.S. Department of State's official website for any updates or changes to the process.

A few years ago, I consulted with a client named "Mariam" from Uzbekistan who had excitedly applied for the DV Lottery. When she was selected, she was overjoyed and reached out for help with the next steps. However, despite repeated reminders, Mariam didn't take the instructions seriously. She submitted her DS-260 form with several inaccuracies, including outdated information about her marital status and education. Worse, she ignored the instructions to bring original documents to her consular interview, showing up instead with only photocopies. The consular officer placed her case under administrative review, and ultimately, her visa was denied due to discrepancies and insufficient documentation. It was heartbreaking, especially because she had a legitimate chance of approval. Mariam's experience is a tough but important lesson: getting selected in the DV Lottery is just the beginning. Careful compliance with every instruction is critical to success.

4. Refugee or Asylum Status

If you have been following the news, it's almost unavoidable to see the term asylum being used when discussing immigration. At the heart of humanitarian immigration is the concept of asylum, which allows individuals who have suffered persecution or have a fear of persecution due to race, religion, nationality, membership in a particular social group, or political opinion to seek safety within the United States

The U.S. asylum system is complemented by the Refugee Admissions Program, which resettles refugees from around the world who have been forced to flee their countries due to conflict, violence, or human rights abuses. Refugee status, unlike asylum, is granted to individuals outside the U.S. who are unable to return to their home country due to persecution.

While it may seem simple to apply, the process is extremely complex and requires careful preparation, thorough documentation, and a clear understanding of the legal requirements and processes.

A significant portion of my firm's work is dedicated to humanitarian-based applications. Asylum is a popular service requested from my office. One common misconception is that applying for asylum is an easy or guaranteed way to stay in the United States, but the reality is far more complex and challenging. I am constantly emphasizing to clients that the asylum process requires applicants to prove they have a well-founded fear of persecution based on race, religion, nationality, political opinion, or membership in a particular social group. One of the common mistakes I see is individuals filing their asylum case on their own, often failing to complete the asylum form properly without any corroborating evidence to support their claim for asylum. Simply put, they believe asylum is filing the form and attending an interview.

Wrong! An asylum case requires proof of the persecution you claim you are suffering, which includes providing official documents to support your claim.

This often involves gathering detailed personal evidence, legal documentation, and, in many cases, undergoing a lengthy legal battle in immigration court. Asylum seekers also face high denial rates, especially without legal representation, and must often wait months or even years for a decision. This process is emotionally and legally demanding and far from a simple or automatic path to legal residency in the U.S

> 💡 **Tip:** You must have authentic documents to prove your asylum/refugee status, or you can be accused of submitting fraudulent documents, barring you from ever receiving a green card in the U.S.

Here are the documents you **must** submit when filing an asylum case:

1. **Personal Statement or Affidavit**: Write a detailed and coherent personal statement describing past persecution and/ or the fear of future persecution. This should include specific incidents, dates, locations, and the impact of these events on your life. The information you provide in this statement must be consistent with the supporting documents you provide and the testimony you provide at the asylum interview.

2. **Supporting Evidence** : Collect and submit documents such as identity papers, medical records, police reports, news articles, and affidavits from witnesses or experts that corroborate your claims. You can also provide Country Conditions, such as reports and articles on the conditions in your home country that support your fear of persecution (e.g., human rights reports, country profiles).

> 💡 **Tip:** Don't wait more than a year to file your application.

The one-year deadline for asylum refers to the requirement that individuals must apply for asylum within one year of their last arrival in the United States. If the applicant misses the one-year deadline and cannot demonstrate an exception, they may be ineligible for asylum.

> 💡 **Tip:** **Preserve your asylee status! (Don't travel to your home country and don't commit crimes.)**

I get this question in almost every asylum consultation I have, and it makes me want to scream in frustration! "How soon can I travel back to my country after I'm approved for asylum?" NEVER! is what I want to yell... but as a professional, I explain the severe legal consequences of getting approved for asylum and then traveling back to the country in which they suffered persecution. Traveling back to your home country after being granted asylum in the United States can jeopardize your asylum status. The grant of asylum is based on the premise that you fear persecution in your home country. Returning to that country could indicate to the U.S. government that your fear of persecution is no longer valid, which might lead to the revocation of your asylum status. If the travel to your home country is deemed voluntary and not due to an extraordinary circumstance, it can be seen as contradicting the basis of your asylum claim.

Even after being granted green card status one year after your asylum approval, traveling to your home country can still be risky. You would have to show extraordinary circumstances for your travel and provide documentation to show those circumstances

5. Special Immigrant Status

Special Immigrant Juvenile Status (SIJS) is a way for certain minors who are in the U.S. and cannot return to their home country to stay in the U.S. legally. It's designed for children who've been abused, neglected, or abandoned by one or both parents. If a child qualifies, they can apply for a green card without needing to go through the regular visa process.

To qualify, the child has to meet specific criteria:

1. They must be under 21 years old.

2. They must be unmarried.

3. A U.S. court must decide that it's not in the child's best interest to return to their home country.

4. They must prove that they've been abused, abandoned, or neglected.

In Special Immigrant Juvenile Status (SIJS) cases, the family court plays a critical role in determining whether a child is eligible for SIJS. Here's a breakdown of what happens in family court:

1. **Filing a Petition**: The petition asks the court to make findings related to the child's situation. Specifically, it seeks a determination that the child has been abused, abandoned, or neglected by one or both parents and that returning to their home country would not be in their best interest. A lawyer or guardian ad litem (someone appointed to represent the child's best interests) will file a petition in family court. Sometimes, it can be filed by a foster parent or other adult who has legal custody of the child.

2. **Court Hearing:** During the hearing, the judge will review evidence (such as affidavits, testimonies, and documents) showing that the child has experienced abuse, abandonment, or neglect. The child might testify, but if they are too young or unable to, other witnesses or experts might provide testimony. The judge must also decide that it is not in the child's best interest to return to their home country, which can involve considering factors like safety, family circumstances, and the child's emotional well-being.

3. **Judge's Findings:**

   ➢ If the court finds that the child meets the criteria for SIJS (abuse, neglect, or abandonment, and not being able to return home), the judge will issue an order that allows the child to apply for SIJS.

   ➢ The court will also issue a **dependency order** or a **custody order**, which helps confirm the child's legal status and living situation.

4. SIJS Recommendation:

> ➤ After the court makes these findings, the order will include an **SIJS recommendation** that is required for the child to apply for lawful permanent residency (a green card).

> ➤ This recommendation is then submitted to U.S. Citizenship and Immigration Services (USCIS) as part of the SIJS application process.

5. Impact of Family Court Order:

> ➤ The family court's ruling doesn't grant the green card itself but is a crucial step in the SIJS process.

> ➤ Once USCIS receives the family court's findings and the child meets all other immigration requirements, the child can apply for a green card through SIJS

6. After the Family Court Decision:

> ➤ The court order might be used to apply for SIJS with USCIS or in immigration court.

> ➤ If a child has been granted SIJS, they can eventually apply for a green card and later pursue citizenship if they meet other qualifications.

SIJS is a great option for minors who are in tough situations and need legal protection to stay in the U.S.

Adjusting Status vs. Consular Processing – To Go or Not to Go, That is the Question

Adjustment of Status is the process for individuals who are **already in the U.S.** on a temporary visa (e.g., tourist, student, or work visa) and are eligible to apply for a green card without having to leave the country. This process allows you to "adjust" your status from a non-immigrant to a lawful permanent resident.

(Aside from parents, spouses and minor children of U.S. citizens, anyone who is not on a valid visa in the U.S. CANNOT adjust status in the U.S. If you are one of those people, you MUST contact an Immigration attorney for advice before starting this process.)

A client named "Jorge" came to me confident that he could adjust his status and get a green card through his U.S. citizen wife. He had entered the country on a visitor visa a year earlier and assumed that his marriage automatically made him eligible for a green card. Unfortunately, during our consultation, it became clear that Jorge had overstayed his visa by several years and had previously re-entered the U.S. without inspection after a brief trip abroad. He didn't realize that this made him inadmissible due to unlawful presence and an illegal re-entry, triggering a permanent bar under immigration law. His case could not move forward without applying for a difficult and rarely granted waiver, and even that required him to leave the U.S.—risking a 10-year bar. Jorge was devastated, not knowing that something as serious as re-entering without inspection could shut the door on his adjustment hopes.

Moral of the story: Assumptions and a lack of legal guidance can lead to heartbreaking outcomes in immigration cases.

If a person is eligible for adjustment of status, he/she is able to file the 'green card application' (I-485) in the U.S., which is sometimes followed by an interview and then issuance of the green card.

Consular Processing is the process for individuals who are **outside the U.S.** or wish to apply for a green card through a U.S. embassy or consulate in their home country. After consular processing, the applicant will enter the U.S. as a permanent resident.

In my years of practicing immigration law, I've often seen clients eager to apply for a green card through adjustment of status simply because they are already in the United States. However, adjustment is not always the best or even a viable option. For many clients, especially those who entered without inspection or have fallen out of status, consular processing may actually be the safer and more appropriate route. While it can be intimidating to leave the U.S. for a consular interview abroad, it is often the only legal pathway available to complete the green card process. I always emphasize to clients that attempting to adjust status without being eligible can lead to denied applications, wasted time and money, and sometimes even removal proceedings. Consular processing, when done correctly and with careful planning, offers a clear and structured path to lawful permanent residence. The key is knowing the risks, preparing thoroughly, and making informed choices based on your specific immigration history.

Chapter 3
Common Pitfalls to Avoid When Filing Your Immigration Case

Filling out your immigration forms might feel like taking the SATs, except you don't get a score report, just the opportunity to wait nervously for months!

A client called my office and consulted with me about submitting his marriage case on his own. He thought he didn't need a lawyer because the process, he thought, was "so straightforward." Fill out some forms, pay the fees and wait for the green card. WRONG. He didn't understand why his case was pending for 3 years. When he showed me a copy of what he submitted, I certainly did. His forms were riddled with mistakes, misspellings, and most importantly, lacked all the supporting documents required for a marriage petition. Worse yet, when I checked the case status online, he was issued a Request for Further Evidence (RFE) from USCIS, which he never received and never answered. Luckily, I was able to request another copy of the RFE and saved his petition from a final denial.

As an immigration attorney, here are some common pitfalls that applicants should avoid when applying for a green card:

1. Inaccurate or Incomplete Information

> **Mistake:** Failing to provide accurate, complete, or truthful information on your application can lead to delays, denials, or even bans from re-entering the U.S.

36

➤ **Solution:** Double-check every detail before submitting. Ensure your application is complete and honest, and that all supporting documents are included. This includes any prior addresses, employment history, or criminal records.

2. Failing to Meet Eligibility Requirements

➤ **Mistake:** Not being fully aware of the eligibility criteria, or failing to meet them, can result in your application being denied.

➤ **Solution:** Make sure you understand whether you qualify under family-based, employment-based, refugee/asylee status, or other green card categories. If you're unsure, consult an immigration lawyer to ensure your eligibility.

3. Missing Deadlines

➤ **Mistake:** Green card applications often have tight deadlines, and missing them can cause your case to be delayed or rejected.

➤ **Solution:** Keep track of all deadlines and ensure timely submission of required documents, applications, and fees. Use a reminder system to stay on top of appointments and deadlines.

4. Not Having the Proper Visa or Status

➤ **Mistake:** Applying for a green card while in the U.S. unlawfully or without proper visa status can trigger serious issues, like deportation.

➤ **Solution:** If you're applying for adjustment of status from within the U.S., ensure you are in a valid immigration status (such as a lawful visitor, student, or fiancé) at the time of application.

5. Ignoring the Medical Exam Requirement

➢ **Mistake:** Failing to undergo the required medical examination by an approved civil surgeon can delay or prevent approval.

➢ **Solution:** Schedule your medical exam early in the process and ensure that an approved doctor does it. Don't wait until the last minute, as it can add weeks to the process.

6. Not Updating USCIS with Address Changes

➢ **Mistake:** Moving without updating your address with USCIS can cause you to miss important notices, such as your interview or decision.

➢ **Solution:** If you move, promptly file a change of address with USCIS and the U.S. Postal Service to ensure that your documents are forwarded correctly.

7. Incorrectly Filing Forms

➢ **Mistake:** Using outdated forms or incorrect versions can result in your application being rejected or delayed.

➢ **Solution:** Always use the most recent versions of the forms, which can be found on the USCIS website. Ensure you're submitting the correct forms for your specific case.

8. Not Disclosing Criminal History

➢ **Mistake:** Failing to disclose past criminal issues, even minor ones, can lead to a denial of your green card application. Certain crimes may make you ineligible for a green card.

➢ **Solution:** Be transparent about your criminal history, including arrests and convictions, and provide all the necessary documentation. If you have concerns, consult an immigration attorney before applying to see how your history may affect your case.

9. Ignoring the Interview Process

➢ **Mistake:** Failing to attend your green card interview or being unprepared can result in the denial of your application.

➢ **Solution:** Be prepared for your interview. Bring all required documents, including any evidence that supports your application. If you're unsure about what's required, ask your attorney for guidance.

10. Not Considering the Impact of Public Charge Rules

➢ **Mistake:** The U.S. has certain "public charge" rules that can make you ineligible for a green card if you are likely to rely on public assistance.

➢ **Solution:** Be prepared to demonstrate that you are financially self-sufficient, either through income, a sponsor, or other financial means. Gather all necessary evidence of financial support.

11. Overlooking the Need for a Valid Passport

➢ **Mistake:** Applying for a green card without having a valid passport or failing to renew an expired one can cause delays or complications.

➢ **Solution:** Ensure your passport is valid for at least six months beyond the date of your green card application. If it's expired or expiring soon, renew it before applying.

12. Not Knowing Your Priority Date and Visa Bulletin

➢ **Mistake:** Many applicants don't track their priority date or check the Visa Bulletin for updates, causing delays or confusion about their status.

➢ **Solution:** Keep track of your priority date and monitor the Visa Bulletin regularly to understand when you can move forward with your green card application, especially if you're applying through a family or employment-based category.

13. Lack of Legal Representation

➢ **Mistake:** Going through the green card process without understanding the complexities can lead to costly mistakes.

➢ **Solution:** If you're unsure about any part of the application or the process, consider seeking legal counsel. Immigration law is complex, and an experienced immigration attorney can guide you through the process and avoid unnecessary errors.

I consulted with a man one time, we'll call him "Raj", who had come to me after applying for his green card. He was in the U.S. working on an H-1B visa. He watched YouTube tutorials and did a lot of "internet research" and felt confident enough to complete his own forms (this is also the type of person who self-diagnoses after asking "Dr. Google" about his symptoms!). As he was completing his forms, he came upon a question - "Have you ever been a member of the totalitarian party?" Raj had no idea what the term meant and didn't bother to look it up, so he decided to check the "Yes" box. Fast forward to the interview. The USCIS officer was scanning his form and paused at the question, confirming that Raj was a member of the totalitarian party. It took a few awkward moments and one very patient USCIS officer before Raj understood that he had declared himself as a threat to democracy in pursuit of permanent residency.

Moral of the story: Double-check your vocabulary before you accidentally admit to being a dictator!

💡 **Tip:** Track your application online using USCIS and NVC portals. Make copies of everything you submit for your personal records. Submit forms in the correct order to avoid processing delays

Chapter 4
Required Documentation

Once you are ready to file for the green card application, whether through adjustment of status or consular processing, some basic documents are always required for all green card applications.

1. Valid passport (including family members)

2. Proof of immigration status

3. Birth certificate

> 💡 **Tip:** **Make sure birth, marriage, and divorce certificates are consistent with the acceptable documents list on the Department of State website (I have included it in Chapter 10).**

4. Proof of Relationship (if family-based) or Proof of Employment (if employment-based)

5. Form I-94 arrival/departure record

6. Proof of Legal Entry

7. Two to Four Passport-sized photos

8. Medical Examination and Vaccination Record

9. Affidavit of Support Form and proof of financial support (discussed later)

10. Police Certificates and Court Records (if applicable)

11. Filing Fees

12. Translations for documents in a foreign language

> 💡 **Tip:** Organize your documents in labeled folders or digital files. Request multiple certified copies of key documents like birth and marriage certificates.

A few years ago, I had a client named "Ahmed" who was filing for his green card through his U.S. citizen wife. He was enthusiastic, polite, and completely unbothered by paperwork, which, as you can imagine, is not ideal in immigration law. When I asked him for his birth certificate, he proudly handed me a laminated piece of paper with cartoon giraffes and rainbows on it. "This," he said confidently, "is the certificate my mom got from the hospital." It turned out to be a decorative birth announcement from a local clinic in his hometown— definitely not an official government-issued document. I explained the difference, and he looked at me, half-laughing, and said, "But it has my footprint on it!" We both laughed, and fortunately, he was able to track down the proper document from his home country a few weeks later.

The Moral of the story: Sentimental value is great, but USCIS prefers official records without giraffes.

Chapter 5
Legal Challenges and How to Overcome Them

Understanding Inadmissibility

When applying for a green card, many applicants are surprised to learn that they may be considered *inadmissible* to the United States, meaning they are ineligible for permanent residency. Inadmissibility can arise for a variety of reasons and prevent applicants from obtaining a green card, even if they meet most of the criteria. Understanding the common grounds for inadmissibility is crucial for anyone seeking permanent residence, as these issues can complicate or even halt the application process. It's important to be aware of these potential barriers before applying and to explore options for overcoming inadmissibility.

Remember my client "Jorge," from Chapter 2? He and his wife were devastated when I had to break the news to him that he would have to return to his home country and could be permanently barred from ever returning to the U.S. These mistakes are made quite often if you don't seek the right advice from an experienced immigration attorney before making any decisions.

So, here are some of the common reasons for inadmissibility:

1. Immigration Violations

> **Unlawful Presence**: Staying in the U.S. beyond the authorized period (overstaying a visa) can lead to inadmissibility. For example, if someone overstays their visa for more than 180 days, they could face a 3-year bar from reentry, and if it exceeds one year, a 10-year bar.

> **Entry Without Inspection**: If someone enters the U.S. without proper documentation or inspection, such as crossing the border without going through customs, they can be considered inadmissible.

> **Violation of Visa Conditions**: Engaging in activities not permitted by your visa (e.g., working on a tourist visa) can lead to inadmissibility.

2. Criminal Convictions

> **Crimes Involving Moral Turpitude (CIMT)**: These are crimes that are considered inherently immoral, such as fraud, theft, or violent crimes. A conviction for a CIMT can result in inadmissibility.

> **Drug Offenses**: A history of drug-related offenses can bar someone from obtaining a green card. Even a conviction for possession of a small number of drugs can lead to inadmissibility.

> **Aggravated Felonies**: Convictions for certain serious crimes, such as murder, trafficking, or violent offenses, can permanently prevent someone from gaining lawful status.

3. Health-Related Grounds

> **Communicable Diseases**: Applicants with certain communicable diseases, such as tuberculosis or syphilis, can be inadmissible unless they show that they are being treated and are no longer a threat.

> **Mental Health Issues**: Some mental health conditions may result in inadmissibility, especially if the person is deemed to be a danger to themselves or others.

> **Lack of Vaccination**: If an applicant has not received the required vaccinations, they may be found inadmissible unless they qualify for an exemption.

4. Public Charge

> **Financial Inability**: If an applicant is determined likely to depend on public assistance or government welfare programs (like food stamps, Medicaid), they can be deemed inadmissible under the "public charge" rule. A sponsor's affidavit of support can sometimes resolve this issue by showing that the applicant will not become a public charge.

5. Fraud or Misrepresentation

> **False Information on Immigration Forms**: Providing false information or fraudulent documents during the application process (e.g., lying about your immigration history or submitting fake marriage certificates) can result in permanent inadmissibility.

> **Misrepresentation of Facts**: If an applicant is found to have willfully misrepresented facts to gain entry or benefits (e.g., entering the U.S. on a tourist visa but intending to stay permanently), they can face serious consequences.

*My client, "Maria", from Brazil, came to the U.S. on a tourist visa to visit family. While here, she met someone, fell in love, and decided to stay longer than planned. But instead of returning home to apply for a correct visa, Maria listened to a friend who told her, "Just say you're here for a quick vacation next time. They never check…" A year later, when she flew back to Brazil for a wedding and then re-entered the U.S. on the same tourist visa, she told the Customs and Border Protection officer that she was only visiting for two weeks. In truth, she planned to stay permanently with her boyfriend. Fast forward a few years. Maria and her boyfriend got married. They filed for her green card, attended the marriage interview, and thought they were nearly done —until the denial letter arrived. USCIS found that Maria had committed **fraud and willful misrepresentation** by lying about her intentions when she reentered the U.S. on her tourist visa. She was inadmissible for adjustment of status. Maria never thought her "white lie" would have these consequences. The road ahead for her and her spouse got much longer and much more complicated – because of one moment of bad advice.*

6. Security and Terrorism-Related Grounds

> ➤ **National Security Concerns**: Applicants who are believed to be involved in activities that threaten the U.S. government, such as espionage, sabotage, or terrorism, are inadmissible.

> ➤ **Affiliation with Terrorist Organizations**: Being affiliated with or supporting a terrorist group can also render someone inadmissible.

7. Prior Immigration Violations

> **Previous Deportation**: If someone has been deported or removed from the U.S. in the past, they could be inadmissible, especially if they did not wait for the required period before reapplying.

> **Multiple Entries After Removal**: Re-entering the U.S. unlawfully after being deported can lead to a permanent ban.

8. Unlawful Employment

> **Unauthorized Employment**: If someone has worked without authorization in the U.S., it can lead to inadmissibility, especially if the person has worked for a significant period without proper work authorization.

9. Immigrant Smuggling

> **Assisting Others to Enter Illegally**: If someone has been involved in smuggling or helping others enter the U.S. illegally, they can be inadmissible.

10. Prior Exclusion or Removal Orders

> **Previous Exclusion or Removal**: If someone was previously excluded or removed from the U.S. and has not waited the required period to reapply (either three years, ten years, or permanent bar), they can be found inadmissible.

If you are met with one of these inadmissibility bars, don't lose hope! It may not be the end of the line for you. There are some options to overcome this, such as applying for a waiver of inadmissibility. The specific waiver will depend on the reason for inadmissibility.

Waivers of Inadmissibility

One of the most difficult parts of my job as an immigration attorney is explaining to a client that they're inadmissible to the United States, but also one of the most rewarding parts is guiding them through the path to a waiver. Many people don't realize they've triggered a ground of inadmissibility, like unlawful presence, fraud, or a past criminal offense, until they're deep into the green card or visa process. Thankfully, there are several types of waivers available, depending on the reason for inadmissibility and the applicant's personal circumstances.

For example, the **I-601A provisional waiver** is designed for people who are inadmissible solely due to unlawful presence and who have a U.S. citizen or lawful permanent resident spouse or parent who would face extreme hardship if they were denied a green card.

I once worked with a client named "Luis," who had entered the U.S. without inspection and lived here quietly for years before marrying his U.S. citizen wife. When he tried to legalize his status, he faced a 10-year bar for unlawful presence. Together, we built a strong I-601A case, showing the medical, emotional, and financial hardships his wife would suffer if he were forced to remain abroad. His waiver was approved, and I still remember the tears in both their eyes when they called me from the airport the day he came home.

In other situations, I help clients apply for the **I-601 waiver**, which is broader in scope. It can be used for unlawful presence, but also for **fraud or misrepresentation**, like using false documents, or for certain **criminal offenses**. One case that stayed with me was "Priya's". She had entered the U.S. with someone else's passport when she was just 17, desperate and scared. Years later, she married a U.S. citizen and tried to apply for a green card, only to be found inadmissible for misrepresentation. We worked closely to prepare her I-601 waiver, documenting the hardship her husband would face if she had to leave and showing her deep remorse and strong community ties. The waiver was granted, and today she's a lawful permanent resident pursuing a degree in nursing.

There are also **212(h) waivers** for certain criminal grounds, and **212(d)(3)** waivers for temporary nonimmigrant visas, where the applicant is inadmissible but needs to come to the U.S. for a short-term purpose. Each waiver is unique—fact-intensive, emotionally demanding, and never guaranteed. But they offer a chance to overcome past mistakes or complex histories. What I've learned from clients like Luis and Priya is that with honesty, good legal strategy, and a strong support system, a waiver can open a door that once seemed permanently closed.

Dealing with Denials and Delays

A denial letter can feel like being told you didn't make the team. But remember: Even Michael Jordan got cut from his high school basketball team. It's not the end, just the beginning of a new play.

As an immigration attorney, one of the most frustrating and, unfortunately, increasingly common challenges I face is helping clients navigate delays and denials from USCIS or the Department of State. I've had cases where green card applications or visa petitions sit untouched for months, sometimes even years, with no clear explanation. For many of my clients, the wait feels like a lifetime, especially for families separated by borders or individuals who see their future on hold. If you find yourself in this situation, my first piece of advice is to be patient, but proactive. While you can't control how long USCIS or the Department of State takes, staying organized and consistently following up can help move things along.

> 💡 **Tip:** **Always keep a detailed log of communication and submission dates. This can help you track the timeline and quickly identify any discrepancies or delays.**

In some cases, if things are dragging on too long, immigration attorneys may be able to file a formal inquiry or even take legal action, like a mandamus lawsuit in federal court, to compel action. As a rule of thumb in my office, if a case has been pending for over a year without an update, I submit an expedited processing request or file a formal inquiry with USCIS or the Department of State.

Dealing with denials can be even more overwhelming. I've represented clients who've been denied for seemingly small mistakes, like a missing signature or submitting the wrong form, but I've also seen denials due to more complex issues, like inadmissibility findings, lack of sufficient evidence, or even accusations of fraud.

One client, "Amina," was denied a fiancé visa after a consular officer questioned the legitimacy of her relationship, despite mountains of proof. In situations like these, it's important to always review the denial letter carefully. It will outline exactly why your case was denied and which evidence may be lacking. In Amina's case, we filed a detailed legal response, addressing every issue raised and providing additional evidence. After months of waiting, her visa was approved.

For clients like "Jorge," whose adjustment of status was denied due to an alleged immigration violation, we were able to file a motion to reopen the case.

One of the most common reasons for denial that I encounter in my practice is when clients fail to respond to a Request for Evidence (RFE) issued by USCIS. An RFE is typically sent when USCIS needs additional information or documentation to make a decision on your case. Unfortunately, I've seen many clients overlook or misunderstand the importance of these requests, leading to denials. This often happens when clients don't fully comprehend the deadline or mistakenly assume that USCIS will reach out again or extend the time.

One client, "Maria", faced a denial for her green card application simply because she missed the deadline to submit the medical exams requested by USCIS. We had been in contact, but she had assumed the request would be automatically extended. When she received the denial, she was devastated, and we had to file a motion to reopen, which prolonged the process.

> 💡 **Tip:** Always pay close attention to the deadlines on RFEs. USCIS typically gives you a window of 30 to 90 days to submit additional documents or evidence, and failing to do so can result in an automatic denial.

If you're facing a denial, don't give up immediately; evaluate whether it's possible to file an appeal or a motion to reopen. You may also be able to file a new application with stronger evidence, especially if your situation has changed. If you're unsure about the next steps, it's essential to consult with a qualified immigration attorney before acting. Mistakes during the appeals or waiver process can make things even more complicated.

Ultimately, the best tip I can give is to stay informed. Immigration law is always evolving, and staying up to date on changes in regulations, processing times, and new forms can help you anticipate potential delays or issues before they arise. And always remember, even when things feel bleak, persistence, careful legal work, and timely follow-ups can turn a difficult situation into a success.

Chapter 6
Navigating Interviews and Biometrics

Preparing for biometrics appointments (fingerprints) and green card interviews is a critical step in the immigration process. Both events are essential for confirming your eligibility for permanent residency, and how you handle them can significantly impact the outcome of your case. As an immigration attorney, I've seen my fair share of clients who were either caught off guard by these events or made simple mistakes that could have been avoided with proper preparation.

Here's what you need to know and some tips to help you succeed.

Biometrics Appointment: What to Expect

The biometrics appointment is usually one of the first steps in the green card process, where you will be required to provide your fingerprints, photograph, and signature for background checks. It's an essential part of verifying your identity and checking for any criminal history or security concerns. While the process itself is relatively straightforward, clients sometimes make the mistake of assuming it's not important. Let me put it this way: it's the only way your case will continue processing.

One of my clients, "Carlos," nearly missed his biometrics appointment because he didn't think it was a big deal. He thought he could simply reschedule later, but that delay ended up setting back his entire application. Show up on time and bring the required documents— usually your appointment notice and a government-issued ID like a passport or driver's license. Missing the appointment without a good reason can lead to a delay or even a denial of your green card application.

Another common mistake I have noticed is clients arriving at the wrong USCIS location. USCIS has specific locations for biometrics appointments, and even though the notice provides the correct address, some clients overlook it. Double-check the address and ensure you're heading to the right USCIS office. Plan to arrive early and expect long lines. The biometrics process usually takes less than an hour, but it's best to give yourself extra time.

Green Card Interview: How to Prepare

I'll start this section with this tip -

Dress appropriately! I won't lie, I sometimes want to punch a hole in the wall when I see clients show up to an interview in a t-shirt and jeans and messy hair, as if they just rolled out of bed for a class they don't want to go to! Other clients come dressed in a full suit. I'd much rather prefer the latter! While there's no official dress code for green card interviews, first impressions matter. Wear professional, neat, clean clothing, as it shows you take the process seriously.

The green card interview is the moment when USCIS officers will evaluate whether your application is legitimate. For family-based applications, they'll often scrutinize the authenticity of your relationship, so it's vital to be prepared to answer questions about how you met your spouse, how long you've been together, and your daily lives as a couple.

I had a client, "Mark," who was applying for a green card through his U.S. citizen wife. They had a solid relationship, but during their interview, Mark struggled to recall important details, like when exactly they got engaged and where they had gone on their first date. Although the officer didn't immediately deny their case, the lack of confidence raised a red flag, and the case was delayed. It is crucial to review your application thoroughly, particularly your responses to relationship-based questions. Be prepared to answer questions confidently and provide any additional evidence that can support your case, like joint bank account statements, photos, or shared insurance policies.

Another client, "Emily," was applying for a green card through her employer. During the interview, she had trouble articulating her current job responsibilities and her role within the company, which led the officer to doubt her employment claim. For employment-based applications, make sure you know the details of your job, including your title, responsibilities, salary, and the company's structure. If you've been promoted or transferred, have documentation to show the changes. It's important to be able to discuss your role clearly and confidently, as inconsistencies can lead to delays or denials.

Be honest and transparent. One of the most damaging things you can do during an interview is to provide false information or try to hide something. USCIS officers are trained to spot inconsistencies, and any attempt to deceive them can lead to serious consequences. And one of the most important things is to breathe! Stay calm. The interview can be nerve-wracking, but it's important to remain calm and composed. Answer questions clearly and concisely, and if you don't know the answer to something, don't be afraid to say so rather than guessing. You can also ask the USCIS officer to clarify the question if you are unsure.

> 💡 **Tip:** Bring all necessary documentation. This includes your passport, appointment notice, copies of forms and documents submitted with your application, and any requested additional documents. Not bringing everything could result in a rescheduled interview, which can delay your case.

Preparing for biometrics and green card interviews may seem intimidating, but with the right mindset and preparation, it can be a smooth and successful part of your immigration journey. My advice is to stay organized, be honest, and practice common questions ahead of time, so you feel confident when the time comes. By avoiding common mistakes and following these tips, you can greatly increase the likelihood of a positive outcome in your immigration process.

Chapter 7
After Approval

Receiving and maintaining your green card

So now that you have the green card, you have to know how to keep it! As an immigration attorney, I can tell you that obtaining a U.S. green card is a complex and tedious process, but what can be even more painful is seeing my clients risk losing it! Although the green card provides privileges and protections similar to U.S. citizens, green card holders are not completely shielded from having their green card taken away if they don't comply with certain rules and responsibilities.

It still baffles me, after so many years of immigration law practice, why USCIS and the Department of State haven't invested in the resources to educate new green card holders on the responsibilities they have in maintaining their legal permanent residence status once they get it. Too many people have reached out to me after being denied entry to the U.S. or have been placed in removal proceedings for violating the "green card rules" simply because they didn't know what they were!

Rights and responsibilities of permanent residents

While a green card grants many rights and benefits, it also comes with certain responsibilities. As a green card holder, you are expected to follow U.S. laws, fulfill certain obligations, and maintain your status as a lawful permanent resident.

Here are the key responsibilities of a green card holder:

1. Obey U.S. Laws

> As a green card holder, you are expected to **follow all federal, state, and local laws**. This includes laws related to criminal conduct, traffic regulations, and civil laws. If you break the law, you could face penalties such as fines, imprisonment, or even deportation. Certain crimes, especially serious ones like drug trafficking or violent offenses, can result in the loss of your green card and removal (deportation) from the U.S.

2. File U.S. Taxes

> **Pay Taxes**: Green card holders are required to **file U.S. income taxes** with the Internal Revenue Service (IRS) every year, just like U.S. citizens. This includes reporting your worldwide income, even if you earn income outside the U.S.

> **Report Foreign Bank Accounts**: If you have financial assets or bank accounts in other countries, you may also need to report them under **FBAR** (Foreign Bank Account Report) requirements.

> Failure to comply with U.S. tax laws can lead to penalties, fines, or even deportation in some cases

3. Maintain Permanent Resident Status (This is a BIG one)

To maintain your green card status, you must live in the U.S. on a permanent basis. You should reside in the U.S. and be physically present for at least six months (180 days) in each calendar year. *And* you need to prove it! This typically includes having ties to the U.S., like employment, property ownership, and family ties.

Staying outside the U.S. for longer than this period may raise questions about abandoning residency.

> **Absences of More Than 6 Months**: If a legal permanent resident is absent from the U.S. for more than 6 months but less than 1 year, they might face scrutiny upon reentry. They will need to prove they did not *intend* to abandon their residency.

> 💡 **Tip:** Keep proof of the reason for your absence from the U.S. for more than 6 months, such as medical documents or a business necessity that required you to be away for that long.

> **Absences of More Than 1 Year:** If you are absent for more than one year, your green card may be considered **abandoned**. These individuals will face issues not only with Customs and Border Protection (CBP) when they are entering at a port of entry, but also will face a difficult time when applying for naturalization.

> 💡 **Tip:** If you have to stay outside of the U.S. for more than a year,obtain a Reentry Permit before leaving the U.S. A Reentry Permit is a special travel document that allows a green card holder to stay outside the U.S. for up to two years without being considered to have abandoned their residency.

I once had a client, "Samir," who got his green card through his U.S. citizen daughter after years of waiting. He was thrilled, relieved even, to finally have lawful permanent resident status in the U.S. But not long after receiving his green card, he made a mistake that nearly cost him everything: he treated it like a visitor visa. Samir had a house, extended family, and business ties back home, so after getting his green card, he returned overseas and stayed there for over a year, thinking he could just "visit" the U.S. every now and then to maintain his status. When he finally returned, CBP officers at the airport pulled him aside and questioned why he had been out of the country so long. He told them honestly that he was only in the U.S. to "visit his daughter for a few weeks." That statement triggered a red flag because green card holders are supposed to live in the U.S. permanently, not use it as a second home or travel base.

He was placed in removal proceedings for having abandoned his residency. We had to fight hard to show that he hadn't intended to give up his permanent residency, gathering evidence of strong U.S. ties and a plan to relocate permanently. Luckily, we were able to convince the immigration judge to give him a second chance, but not without months of stress and legal fees. The lesson? A green card is not a long-term visitor visa; it's a commitment to make the U.S. your permanent home. If you're not ready for that, you may be better off applying for a visitor visa until you are.

4. Notify USCIS of Address Changes

> ➢ You are required to inform the **U.S. Citizenship and Immigration Services (USCIS)** of any address changes within **10 days** of moving. This is done by filing Form **AR-11** (Alien's Change of Address).

> Failure to update your address could lead to missing important notices or delays in your green card renewal or immigration processing.

5. Carry Proof of Your Green Card

> Green card holders must **carry proof** of their status as permanent residents, especially when traveling or dealing with immigration authorities. You should always have your **green card** with you or be able to prove your legal status if requested by law enforcement or immigration officers.

> 💡 **Tip:** Keep your green card in a secure place, but carry a photocopy for emergencies. If you have an attorney, make sure the attorney has a copy of the FRONT and BACK of the green card.

6. Register for Selective Service (if applicable)

> **Men between the ages of 18 and 25** who are green card holders are required to register with the **Selective Service System**. This is the system used by the U.S. government to maintain a list of people eligible for a military draft in case of a national emergency. Registration is a legal requirement, and failure to comply can affect your ability to become a U.S. citizen later.

7. Green Card Renewal or Replacement

> Green cards are not permanent documents; they must be **renewed** every **10 years**. It's your responsibility to apply for renewal well before the expiration date (usually within 6 months).

> ➤ If your green card is lost, stolen, or damaged, you must apply for a **replacement** by filing a replacement form with USCIS.

💡 **Tip:** Use tools like email reminders or apps to track green card renewal deadlines.

---

8. Avoid Committing Fraud or Misrepresentation

> ➤ Any attempt to **commit fraud** or **misrepresentation** during the green card application process or during your time as a green card holder can result in the **revocation of your green card** and potential deportation.

> ➤ Misrepresentations about your status, such as providing false information or documentation to gain benefits, can severely impact your ability to remain in the U.S. or apply for U.S. citizenship in the future.

9. Notifying USCIS of Criminal Convictions

> ➤ Green card holders must notify USCIS if they are convicted of certain crimes. Certain criminal convictions can lead to deportation, so it's essential to stay in compliance with U.S. criminal laws.

> ➤ Green card holders should **avoid criminal activity**, as a conviction for serious crimes may render them ineligible for U.S. citizenship and could lead to the loss of their green card.

10. No Voting in Federal Elections (Another BIG ONE)

➤ Green card holders **cannot vote** in federal elections (for president, U.S. Congress, or senators). Only U.S. citizens have the right to vote in these elections.

➤ **State and local elections**: Some states may allow green card holders to vote in certain **local elections** (such as for city council or school boards), but this is rare, and you must check local laws for eligibility.

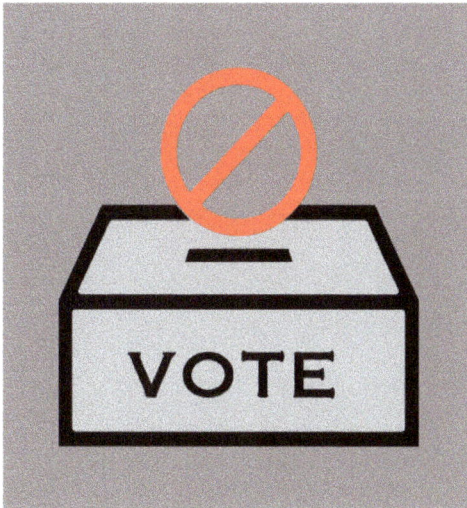

11. Apply for U.S. Citizenship (Optional)

➤ While not a responsibility, **green card holders are encouraged to apply for U.S. citizenship** once they meet the eligibility requirements (typically after 5 years as a permanent resident, or 3 years if married to a U.S. citizen). We'll discuss this in the next chapter.

12. Abide by Restrictions on Certain Activities

> ➤ Some activities or behaviors can lead to the **revocation of your green card.** For example:

- ○ **Polygamy**: Green card holders cannot engage in polygamous marriages.

- ○ **Terrorist Activities or Subversive Actions**: Engaging in activities that pose a threat to U.S. national security can lead to removal proceedings.

- ○ **Illegal Voting**: Voting in federal elections or other prohibited elections as a green card holder is illegal.

Chapter 8
Preparing for the Next Step:
U.S. Citizenship

Even though this book is primarily about obtaining and keeping a green card, I thought it would be important to provide you with information about the ultimate goal- **becoming a U.S. citizen**!

Benefits of becoming a U.S. citizen

Becoming a U.S. citizen comes with a lot of perks, and it may also simplify some aspects of immigration, including traveling and renewing documents. One of the biggest benefits is the right to vote, which means you get to have a say in who leads the country and your local community. You also gain access to job opportunities that are only open to citizens, including some government positions that require security clearance.

Traveling becomes a lot easier, too, as a U.S. passport allows you to visit many countries without needing a visa, and you can count on support from U.S. Embassies if you run into trouble abroad (green card holders get this benefit, too).

In my opinion, one of the greatest benefits that citizenship also provides is protection from deportation. Having citizenship means not having to worry about losing your legal status, which we previously said can happen to a green card holder, especially when faced with legal issues.

"Carlos" came to the U.S. as a teenager, worked hard and eventually became a green card holder. One night, he made a mistake – got into a fight and ended up with an assault charge. Although it wasn't a serious offense, he soon found himself facing possible deportation. That's when he realized how vulnerable his status was, even after living in the country for over a decade. Determined to secure his future, Carlos worked with my office to apply for citizenship as soon as he became eligible. A few years later, as a proud U.S. citizen, he knew that a similar mistake wouldn't threaten his right to stay in the country. Gaining citizenship gave him a sense of security and peace of mind, knowing that his life in the U.S. was truly permanent.

💡 **Tip:** If you have a criminal record when applying for citizenship, it's important to discuss it with an immigration attorney BEFORE applying, since certain crimes can affect the good moral character requirement for citizenship and prevent your eligibility to become a citizen.

When and how to apply for Naturalization

"Naturalization" is the term used to explain the process of obtaining U.S. citizenship. It's probably the most exciting time for me and my clients when they begin this process, as if they are almost at the finish line!

But as I always tell my clients, citizenship is a privilege and not a right! What this means is that you must be eligible to apply for citizenship, and you cannot just apply for it because you completed the time period needed, as discussed below. I cannot begin to tell you how often I get a call from a potential client telling me their application was denied because they were not eligible! And yes, USCIS will accept the application, take the fee, schedule you for your appointment, interview you AND THEN TELL YOU YOU'RE NOT ELIGIBLE! It's very disappointing and completely avoidable if you speak with an immigration attorney first before applying.

*"Rico," a charming but slightly overconfident man from Italy, had lived in the U.S. for a grand total of **three months** when he marched into a USCIS office, convinced he was ready to become a U.S. citizen.*

Officer Smith: "Sir, you need to have lived in the U.S. as a permanent resident for at least five years before applying for naturalization."

Rico: "Ah, but I've been here for three months, and let me tell you— I have done more American things in that time than most people do in a lifetime!"

Officer Smith: "Oh, really?"

Rico: "Absolutely! I've been to a monster truck rally, eaten a deep-fried Twinkie, got into a heated debate about which BBQ style is superior, AND I say 'y'all' now. I even started complaining about taxes and Wi-Fi speed! If that's not American, I don't know what is."

Officer Smith (chuckling): "Impressive... but rules are rules."

Rico: "Okay, okay... what if I marry an American? That speeds things up, right?"

Officer Smith: "It does, but you need to be married for three years and live together."

Rico: "Three years?! What if I marry three Americans? Does it add up?"

Needless to say, Rico's application was denied, but he left the office with a USCIS officer laughing and a new plan: opening an authentic Italian food truck while patiently waiting out his five years.

Moral of the story: Living like an American doesn't make you a citizen... but it sure makes for a good time!

So, let's discuss what those eligibility requirements are:

1. Age Requirement

> ➤ You must be **at least 18 years old**; children who are under the age of 18 acquire U.S. citizenship from a U.S. citizen parent without going through the entire naturalization process.

2. Lawful Permanent Resident (Green Card Holder)

> ➤ You must have a **green card (permanent resident status)** for at least:
>
>   o **5 years** (if applying as a regular permanent resident).

- o **3 years** (if you received your green card through marriage to a U.S. citizen AND are still married to that U.S. citizen)

3. Continuous Residence & Physical Presence

- ➤ **You must** have lived **continuously** in the U.S. for the required time.

- ➤ **You must** have been **physically present** in the U.S. for at least **30 months out of the last 5 years** (or **18 months out of 3 years** if married to a citizen).

4. Good Moral Character

- ➤ **You must** have no serious **criminal offenses.**

- ➤ **You must** follow **U.S. laws** and be of good ethical standing.

5. English Language Proficiency

- ➤ **You must** be able to **read, write, and speak basic English** (some exemptions apply for older applicants with long residency).

6. U.S. Civics Test

- ➤ **You must** pass a **test on U.S. history and government** (unless exempt due to age or disability).

7. Oath of Allegiance

- ➤ **You must** take the **Oath of Allegiance** to the U.S. to complete the process.

> 💡 **Tip:** Don't wait for the three/five years to pass to begin preparing for naturalization. You can apply up to 90 days before the period ends, so start gathering documents early and reach out to an immigration attorney!

A client came to me to apply for citizenship. He disclosed that he was convicted of one domestic violence charge. During the course of the consultation, I pressed the client a little more about his criminal record. I advised him that disclosing all crimes for which he was charged, arrested, OR convicted needed to be disclosed to me because it wasn't in his best interest to keep it from me. He finally told me that he had also been arrested and charged for domestic violence, which happened before his other conviction, but that the charges were eventually dismissed. I explained to him that ALL charges, arrests and convictions had to be disclosed. But more importantly, the two charges could negatively impact a "good moral character" finding for purposes of citizenship. Ultimately, I advised him to hold off on filing and build a strong case to show his good character and rehabilitation, like a letter from his employer, statements from his friends and family, or his volunteer work. The client was upset because he was looking forward to filing, but LUCKILY listened to my advice.

I'm happy to share that the client is now a U.S. citizen!

Chapter 9
FAQs and Practical Advice

One of the most rewarding parts of being an immigration attorney is answering the questions that clients (and prospective applicants) have about the green card process. Some questions pop up over and over again. While the answers can be long, complex, or full of nuance, there are a few that always seem to stand out. Let's dive into some of the most commonly asked ones, and I'll try to break them down in a way that's easy to understand.

1. How long does it take to get a green card?

Ah, the million-dollar question! The honest answer is it depends. For some, it's a matter of months; for others, it can take years. The timeline varies based on factors like your immigration category (family-based, employment-based, refugee/asylee, etc.), your country of origin (countries like India or Mexico may have longer wait times), and whether you're applying from within the U.S. or from abroad. Keep in mind that it's not just about paperwork; it's also about processing times and the availability of visa numbers.

2. What's the difference between a green card and a visa?

Think of a visa like a temporary ticket to the U.S. It allows you to visit, work, or study here for a certain period of time. But a green card? That's the golden ticket to permanent residency. With a green card, you can live and work in the U.S. indefinitely, and it opens the door to eventually applying for citizenship, if you wish.

3. What happens if I make a mistake on my application?

First, don't panic! Mistakes happen, but they can cause delays or complications. If you realize you've made an error before submitting, you can correct it. If you catch it after you've already filed, you may need to file an amended form or provide additional evidence. The key is to be proactive. If in doubt, consult an attorney who can guide you through the process to fix any mistakes.

4. Do I have to be in the U.S. when I apply?

Not necessarily. You can apply for a green card while you're abroad, through a process called consular processing. This involves a U.S. consulate in your home country. If you're already in the U.S., you can apply through adjustment of status, which means you're applying to change your immigration status while staying inside the country.

5. Can my spouse or children come with me on my green card?

Yes! If you're granted a green card, your immediate family (spouse and unmarried children under 21) can apply for green cards as derivative applicants, usually at the same time or shortly after you. Just make sure to include them in your application and provide the necessary documentation.

Practical Tips for Staying Organized and Informed

The green card process can feel like a marathon, but with a little preparation and organization, it doesn't have to be a total nightmare. Here are a few tips to help you stay on top of the mountain of paperwork and keep your sanity intact.

1. Create a Green Card Checklist

Start by making a detailed checklist of everything you need to do. Breaking down the process into manageable steps helps you avoid missing deadlines. The checklist should include:

- ➢ Forms to fill out (e.g., I-485, I-130)
- ➢ Supporting documents (e.g., birth certificates, proof of employment)
- ➢ Any medical exams or biometrics appointments
- ➢ Interview prep (if required)

And don't forget to check them off once they're done!

2. Keep Your Documents in One Place

The more organized you are, the smoother the process will go. Create a folder (physical or digital) to store all the documents related to your green card application. Keep copies of everything you submit to USCIS, as well as any correspondence you receive from them. You'll be surprised how often you'll need to refer to those documents again.

3. Set Calendar Reminders

A lot of people overlook the importance of deadlines, especially if the processing time stretches over a year or more. Set reminders for things like:

- ➢ Interview dates
- ➢ When to submit additional evidence or documents
- ➢ Renewal dates for temporary work permits or travel authorizations.

These little reminders can prevent you from missing crucial deadlines.

4. Stay Calm and Patient

Yes, easier said than done! But remember, the green card process is rarely a sprint. There are often long waiting periods, and some things are out of your control. Keep your chin up and try not to stress too much over the timeline. It's important to stay informed and proactive, but equally important to stay patient.

Understanding the Role of Legal Representation

I get asked a lot whether hiring an immigration lawyer is necessary. While the process is something that many people can handle on their own—especially if their case is simple—having legal representation can make a huge difference, particularly if things get complicated. (Many of my clients tell me that one of the biggest benefits of having me as their lawyer is the peace of mind they gain, knowing that their future is in the hands of an experienced professional.)

An immigration attorney can help you:

➤ **Navigate Complex Legal Requirements**: U.S. immigration law is *complex*, and one small mistake can set you back months or even years. An attorney will make sure all the documents are filed correctly, and they'll know the ins and outs of your specific case.

➤ **Prepare You for the Interview**: For many applicants, the green card interview is the most stressful part of the process. An attorney can help you understand what to expect and prepare you to answer questions confidently.

➤ **Resolve Issues**: If you're facing a denial, an attorney can help you assess your options and file an appeal or a waiver if necessary. They can also help if you've experienced delays or complications that need extra attention.

➤ **Avoid Costly and Sometimes Heartbreaking Mistakes**: An attorney ensures your application is accurate, complete and submitted on time. They can spot potential issues early and guide you through every step of the process. With professional support, you reduce the risk of delays, rejections, or deportation, protecting your future and peace of mind.

In short, while you can likely navigate the process on your own if you're comfortable, a good immigration attorney is like a personal guide through the legal maze. And, in my opinion, it's an investment (and a type of **"insurance policy"**) seriously worth considering.

Tips & Tricks:

1. Join Online Immigration Forums for Peer Advice (but Verify with Official Sources)

The internet is full of forums and online communities where applicants share their experiences and advice. These platforms can be great for finding moral support and learning from others who've been through the process.

Be cautious: not all advice is created equal. Forums often have well-meaning but inaccurate information. Always verify anything you read with official sources like the USCIS website or, better yet, consult an immigration lawyer.

2. Stay Updated on Immigration Policy Changes

Immigration policy is constantly evolving, and changes can affect your green card process. Subscribe to trusted news outlets, follow USCIS updates, or sign up for newsletters that focus on immigration law. You don't want to be caught off guard by a new rule or regulation that could impact your application.

Reliable resources include:

> **USCIS.gov** for updates on processing times, new forms, and policy changes.

> **American Immigration Lawyers Association (AILA)** for professional insights and guidance.

> **Immigration News Websites** (like Immigration Law Help) to stay on top of broader legal trends.

Being informed means you're not just following the process, you're staying ahead of it.

Chapter 10
Resources and Contacts

In the world of immigration law, knowledge is power. Whether you're just starting your green card journey or are in the middle of your application, it's crucial to have reliable resources at your fingertips. In this chapter, I'll provide a list of websites and contact information that I've found to be most useful for anyone dealing with the green card process.

1. U.S. Citizenship and Immigration Services (USCIS)

➢ **Website:** www.uscis.gov

➢ **What You'll Find**: The official government website for all things immigration. It's the primary source for information about the green card process, from eligibility criteria to application forms and instructions. You can check processing times, track the status of your application, and find official updates on policy changes.

> 💡 **Tip:** **Always start here for the most current and authoritative information on your case.**

2. Department of State – Bureau of Consular Affairs (Visa Services)

➢ **Website:** www.travel.state.gov

➢ **What You'll Find**: If you're applying for a green card from abroad (through consular processing), this is the official site for all U.S. visa-related matters. It provides details on visa categories, the interview process, and country-specific requirements.

> 💡 **Tip:** Use the Visa Bulletin to check the availability of visa numbers, especially if you're from a country with a high demand for green cards.

3. U.S. Department of Labor (Employment-Based Green Cards)

> ➢ **Website**: www.dol.gov

> ➢ **What You'll Find**: If you're applying for a green card based on employment (through the EB-1, EB-2, or EB-3 categories), this site provides information on labor certification, employer requirements, and job market tests.

> 💡 **Tip:** If you're an employer seeking to sponsor a green card, this site will be invaluable for understanding your responsibilities and the legal process.

4. Visa Bulletin (Check wait times for family and employment-based cases)

> ➢ **Website:** www.travel.state.gov/content/travel/en/legal/visa-law0/visa-bulletin.html

> ➢ **What You'll Find**: The Visa Bulletin is published by the Department of State every month and shows the availability of green cards for people from different countries and in different categories. It is an essential tool for tracking when your green card will become available based on your priority date and country of origin.

> 💡 **Tip:** Bookmark this page, as you'll need to refer to it often to understand whether you can move forward with your application or whether you need to wait for a visa number to become available.

5. U.S. Immigration and Customs Enforcement (ICE)

➤ **Website**: www.ice.gov

➤ **What You'll Find**: While ICE is not directly involved in the green card application process, it plays a role in immigration enforcement. This site can be useful for learning about your rights as an immigrant and understanding how to avoid potential issues that could affect your green card status, like violations of immigration laws.

> 💡 **Tip:** If you're worried about your immigration status or enforcement issues, it's important to stay informed about ICE policies and understand how they may affect you.

6. USCIS Online Account

➤ **Website:** www.my.uscis.gov

➤ **What You'll Find**: This portal allows you to create a personal USCIS account where you can check the status of your green card application, file forms online, and receive notifications about your case.

> 💡 **Tip:** Create an account early in the process to track your application, make sure your contact information is up to date, and receive notifications on any updates or requests for additional documents.

Other Useful Resources

➢ **U.S. Citizenship Test Prep**:

- o **Website**: www.uscitizenpod.com

- o **What You'll Find**: If you're applying for citizenship after getting your green card, this site offers study materials for the U.S. citizenship test.

➢ **Social Security Administration (SSA)**

- o **Website**: www.ssa.gov

- o **What You'll Find**: If you need to apply for a Social Security Number (SSN) as part of your green card process, this site will guide you through the application process and provide information on benefits for immigrants.

Contacting USCIS or Other Agencies

If you ever need to contact USCIS directly, you can:

➢ **Call USCIS Customer Service**: 1-800-375-5283

(TDD for the hearing impaired: 1-800-767-1833)

➢ **Make an Appointment**: If you need an in-person appointment, use the **InfoPass** system to schedule an appointment at a local USCIS office.

With the right resources and contacts, you can keep your green card process on track and avoid unnecessary confusion. Remember, you don't have to go through this journey alone—many tools and organizations can help you every step of the way. Make sure you rely on trusted sources, stay organized, and always seek legal counsel if you're unsure about any part of the process.

https://www.senate.gov/senators/senators-contact.htm

https://www.house.gov/representatives/find-your-representative

> ➢ Many **Congressional offices** have a department that helps constituents with immigration delays. They can **contact USCIS directly** on your behalf and may speed up your case.

> 💡 **Tip:** If your case is delayed or you believe there is a problem, and you have exhausted all the possible ways to move your case, it's recommended to contact your local congressional office for help

Conclusion

Keep Going—The Green Card Journey is Worth It

Let's be real for a second: navigating the green card process is no walk in the park. I've seen it all—clients who start the process with excitement, then hit a wall of paperwork and confusion. I've also seen the complete opposite, clients who start out completely overwhelmed but end up crossing that finish line with a sense of pride, relief, and a big smile on their faces. That's why I do what I do—to help you get there.

Stay Confident, Stay Proactive

I remember one client, "Sozan," who came to me years ago. She'd already tried to file her green card application on her own and had gotten tangled in a series of mistakes. She was frustrated and ready to give up. But after sitting down with her, reviewing her documents, and setting up a clear action plan, we got her application back on track. Just a few months later, she called me, almost in tears, when she got her green card approval notice. It was one of the happiest phone calls I've ever received.

Sozan's story isn't unique. I've seen so many people make huge strides, sometimes just by understanding the process better, staying organized, or simply getting the right advice at the right time. And that's the key here: **you don't have to go through this alone.** The green card process is complicated, but with the right tools, resources, and support, you can do it. So, take a deep breath, stay proactive, and remember that every form you fill out and every document you submit is one step closer to your goal.

A Few Final Words from Me

I've spent practically my entire legal career navigating the immigration maze, and let me tell you, I've had my fair share of "what on earth is going on?" moments. When I first started practicing law, I thought I knew everything until my first green card case hit my desk. The paperwork alone felt like an entire library of forms, and I quickly realized there was so much I didn't know. But over time, I've learned that the key to success is staying informed, being organized, and above all, asking for help when needed.

The green card process is like assembling a massive puzzle. Some pieces fit right away, and others require more time and patience. But just like that moment when the final piece clicks into place, the feeling of receiving your green card is one of pure joy. I've seen the smiles, the sighs of relief, and the celebrations. And that's why I'm here: to guide you through it and help you achieve that goal.

> 💡 **Pro Tip:** Focus on the Long-Term Goal

Let's finish with a little advice from someone who's been in the trenches. When you're deep into filling out forms and waiting for processing times, it's easy to lose sight of the bigger picture. It's easy to get frustrated. But take it from me, **every step forward counts.** Think of this process like a road trip. You're not going to get to your destination in a single leap. There will be detours, speed bumps, and maybe even a flat tire or two (believe me, I've had my share). But if you stay the course, keep moving, and focus on the long-term goal, you'll get there.

And here's the truth: **Getting your green card is not just about paperwork, it's about your future.** It's about being able to live, work, and build a life in the United States. That's a powerful thing. Don't rush it, and don't get discouraged. Every small step brings you closer to the life you've been dreaming of.

I'm Here for You

If you're feeling lost, stuck, or just need someone to help you make sense of the process, don't hesitate to reach out. As an immigration attorney, I've dedicated my career to helping people like you navigate the green card journey. I've been through this process countless times, both personally (as the daughter of immigrants) and professionally. If you need guidance or simply someone who *gets it*, I'm here to help.

Remember, you don't have to do this alone. Whether you need help with a complicated form, have questions about your eligibility, or just need some moral support, I'm just a phone call or email away.

Reach out to me, and together we can get you across that finish line. Call me for a consultation, mention this book, and I'll give you a special bonus, just as a thank you.

Best of luck, and here's to your bright future ahead in the United States of America!

Appendix

Appendix A

Green Card Approval Notice

Receipt Number

Date needed to check for the visa bulletin

Green card category

USCIS Service Center

Appendix B

I-551 MRIV

Appendix C

ADJUSTMENT OF STATUS
vs. CONSULAR PROCESSING

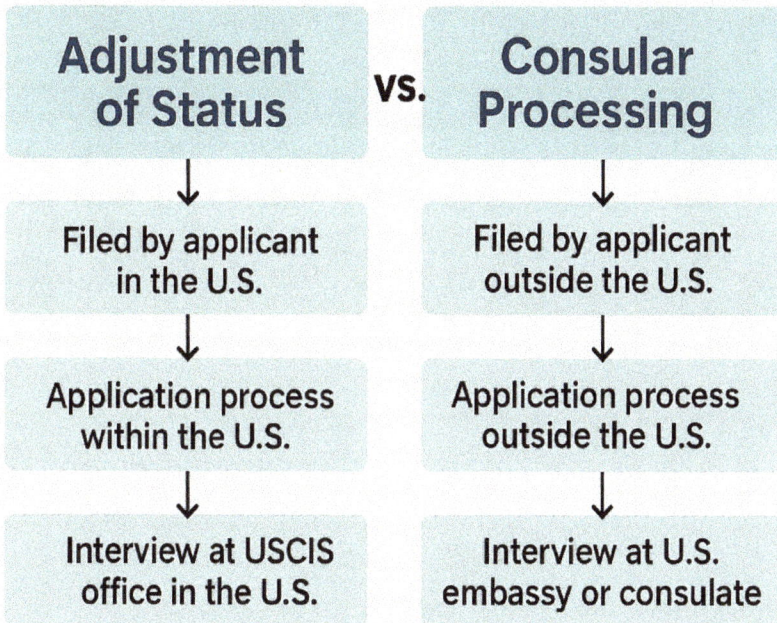

Adjustment of Status	vs.	Consular Processing
↓		↓
Filed by applicant in the U.S.		Filed by applicant outside the U.S.
↓		↓
Application process within the U.S.		Application process outside the U.S.
↓		↓
Interview at USCIS office in the U.S.		Interview at U.S. embassy or consulate

Appendix D

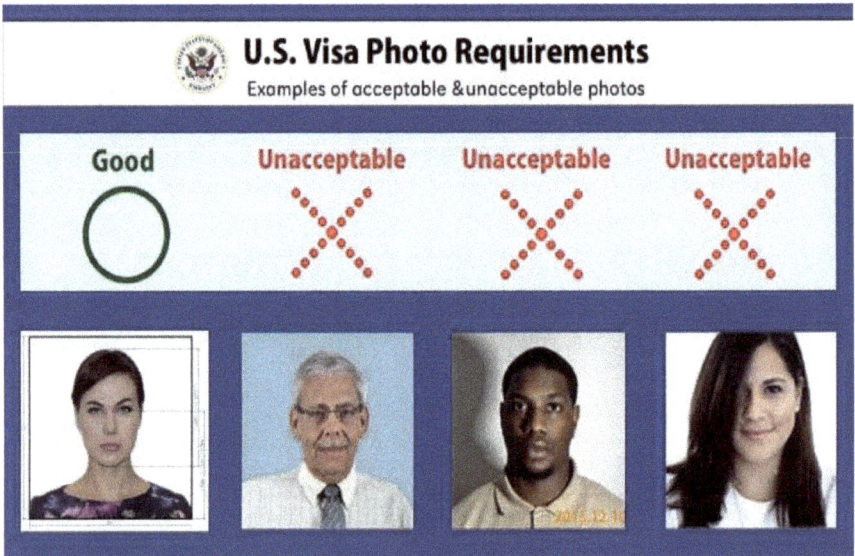

U.S. Visa Photo Requirements
Examples of acceptable & unacceptable photos

Good | Unacceptable | Unacceptable | Unacceptable

i. The photo is sized 51 x 51 mm.

ii. Your head is between 1 and 1 ⅜ inches (22 mm and 35 mm) or 50% and 69% of the image's total height from the bottom of your chin to the top of the head.

iii. The photo was taken within the last six months.

iv. The photo is in full color.

v. The background is plain white.

vi. There are no shadows in the photo.

vii. You are facing the camera straight-on and not at an angle.

viii. Your facial expression is neutral.

ix. Your eyes are open.

x. You are not wearing eyewear unless required for medical reasons. Glasses that are permitted for medical reasons must not have any glare or shadows.

xi. You are not wearing any electronic devices such as headphones. Hearing devices or similar devices required for medical reasons are allowed.

xii. You are wearing 'everyday clothing' and not, for example, a uniform.

xiii. Your hairline is visible, and your head is not covered unless it is a headdress for religious reasons. Headdresses must not cover the face.

1-800 946-LAWUSA

Info@sedkilaw.net

www.sedkilaw.com

www.ingramcontent.com/pod-product-compliance
Lightning Source LLC
Chambersburg PA
CBHW052119030426
42335CB00025B/3048